Rosary of Bones

09-07

For Marilyn
with affection & the pleasure
of meeting one of Peggy's
old friends —
Best,
Jenny

Rosary of Bones

Poems by Jennifer MacPherson

Cherry Grove Collections

Published by Cherry Grove Collections
P.O.Box 541106
Cincinnati, OH 45254-1106

Poetry Editor: Kevin Walzer
Business Editor: Lori Jareo

ISBN: 9781933456799
LCCN: 2007933295

Cover Art: "Climbing Rose" oil painting by Colin Page

Visit us on the web at www.cherry-grove.com

Acknowledgments

Grateful acknowledgment is made to the editors of the following periodicals and anthologies in which these poems first appeared: *Angel Face:* "Early April, Washington Heights"; *Asheville Poetry Review*: "What Happens in September"; *Blue Unicorn*: "The Bone Poem"; *Blue Violin:* "Her Father's Last Visit"; *Buckle &:* "Rosary of Bones"; *The Café Review:* "Crows Are Fighting in the Trees Again"; *Calyx*: "Credo"; *Clackamas Literary Review*: "Fifty-Fifth Birthday Blues"; *Coevolution: The MNP 2006 Anthology:* "Making Music, NYC, Early 20th Century"; *The Comstock Review:* "80 Degrees Fahrenheit and the Geese Are Crying," "As October Ends," "Christmas Eve," "Flying to Maine," "Grandmother and the Barrel of Rattlers," "Late Night, Late September," "My Life with Birds" (as "To Write About Birds"), "This is not a new unhappiness," "Three Hundred and Sixty Degrees," "Why I Am a Poet," "X-ray" (as "Glow"); *The Connecticut Review*: "Singing at the Execution"; *Connecticut River Review:* "Destinations"; *The Distillery:* "Derecho" (as "They Called It Derecho"); *Emrys Journal:* "History Class"; *Louisiana Literature:* "Carrying the Dead," "Dinner for One: Detroit," "Portrait of an Unknown Girl"; *Lucid Moon (Web):* "Thirty Years Have Not Passed," "Visiting My In-Laws," "Why I Cannot Give the Piano Away"; *Mad Poets Review*: "Before My Bones Were Set"; *Main Street Rag:* "Above the Dresser," "Charlotte Fears for Her Son," "Dinner for One: Philadelphia," "Ethel and Julius" (as "Goin' Fishin', 1953"), "My Ex-Boyfriend Takes out the Garbage," "The Woman Down the Street"; *Mobius*: "Necessary Homework"; *Monkey's Fist*: "Connie Recounts Her Dreams to the Therapist"; *Northwest Florida Review:* "Waiting for the Ferry"; *Northwoods Journal*: "First Glimpsed Under a Bathroom Lamp," "Summer 1963" (as "Stepping Back to Summer 1963"); *Plainsongs*: "Barren"; *Poetry International*: "Physical Examination"; *Red Wheelbarrow:* "The Cutting Edge"; *The Seasons:* "Moment of Truth"; *Small Pond Magazine of Literature:* "Lost Babies"; *South Carolina Review:* "Menopause in March"; *Sulphur River Review*: "Autumn Bones," "Birds At Rest," "Massachusetts Landscape," "Nineteen Fifty One,"

"Photo Found Caught in the Back of a Drawer," "Putting It in Perspective"; *Visions International*: "Throwing the Bones."

"Before My Bones Were Set," "Nineteen Fifty One," and "Ethel and Julius" (as "Goin' Fishin' 1953,") also appeared in a chapbook, *Stuck in Time* (Pudding House, 2002). "The Bone Poem," "Charlotte Fears for Her Son," "Lost Babies," and "Christmas Eve" also appeared in the chapbook *Jennifer MacPherson's Greatest Hits* (Pudding House, 2001). "The Bone Poem" was also featured in *Primary Care Geriatrics: A Case-Based Approach, 4th Edition* (Morley: R. Ham, R. Sloane, P. and Warshaw, G. eds.). "Physical Examination" also previously appeared in *In the Mixed Gender of the Sea* (Spire Press, 2004). "Waiting for the Ferry" was reprinted in *Taproot*. "Crows Are Fighting in the Trees Again" was reprinted in *The Clackamas Review* and in *The Friends of Acadia Journal*. "Fifty-Fifth Birthday Blues" was reprinted in *The Café Review*. "Dinner for One: Detroit" was a semi-finalist for the 2000 Emily Dickinson award and was reprinted in the *Emily Dickinson Anthology 2000*.

Many thanks to those who have helped in the creation and refinement of poems in this collection, especially Madeleine Crouse, Frank Johnson, Molly Peacock, Bruce Weigl, Michael Dennis Browne, the talented and supportive members of the Syracuse Woman's Poetry Group, the Fourth Wednesday Poetry Group, the members of the Ithaca Day Group and, never forgotten, the love and emotional support generously given by the Comstock Writers' Group, especially Peg Flanders, Peggy Miller, and the late Ann Silsbee. I want to say a special thank-you to Sallie Bailey for her help in book design, to the wonderful young artist Colin Page whose art illuminates the front cover, to Donna M. Davis, typesetter extraordinaire, and to Kevin Walzer and Lori Jareo of WordTech for all they do for poetry.

For my sisters of choice: Kathleen, Peg, Yvonne, Joanie, and Priscilla

and in memory of my family of origin

Table of Contents

Credo

I believe in the testament of bones, their tensile strength.
Little girls jumping rope, boys with hockey sticks,
leap moons every day. They whirl like planets
and their bones turn the wheel of the universe.

I believe in the torso, ankles, spine, and those small
sticky ribs. I rejoice in my bones each morning,
rise from bed on legs that hold me straight,
walk me to the kitchen. I lift my coffee cup
with a slender filigree of fingers. My hat
fits my skull and I dare the world with my chin.

At night, my bones retract into a thin skin of dreams.
These, too, I believe. An undercut of sorrow
runs beneath. I accept the slow dissolve into mineral.
I touch my knees, my breastbone, feel the outward scars,
believe that mysteries are happening deeper than skin;
so soon bones diminish and fall away.

I believe nothing is wasted: calcium-crumble,
grate of shale, arrowheads once lost now found,
even shiny leaves, the pointed blades of grass.
Everything that has moved in the rain.

The Bone Poem

for Yvonne

Bones
waken me to midnight's open silence
with their ghostly ache,
suggest that it's time to bargain again with god

not the God of meek and gentle heart
who rises – perfect – each Spring
but an older, arthritic god
who knows about bones,
notes the hour
when they begin to slowly grind each other,
when skin thins and they stand like
so many knobby sentinels.

This god counts poems
we have yet to write
like a rosary of bones clicking
through his gnarled fingers,
naming each one as it begins to split:
tibia, fibula, radius, ulna.

Older than benevolence,
this is the god
who shatters stone in rage,
who makes seas swallow regiments,
whose own bones mutter when he leans to listen.

Dinner for One: Detroit

That day I fell sick with a cold, so sick
I stayed back at the Residence Inn,
watched courtroom tv all day, all the sleazy
dailiness of detail spread for the public slaver,
huddled, pink flannelette nightie
bunched around my calves to keep warm.
By five, I'd had enough. The manager said
the Big Fish Two stood "only three buildings away,"
(each lot equal to a fair-sized city block). Rain whipped
my coat, wind slammed its fist to my face, the flooded walks
posed barricades of water surrounded by swamp. I
arrived chilly and shivering, feet soaked.

The restaurant was decorated for Christmas:
red flowered tablecloths, crimson velvet bows
looped everywhere. At a little past five, only a few
had braved the rainy Detroit dark. In a cozy booth, I
was cosseted with hot bread and red wine, salad
of red and green leaf lettuce, pine nuts, red onion
and blue cheese dressed with raspberry vinaigrette,
broiled falling-apart crab cakes with Bearnaise sauce,
sugar-snap peas, glossy butter-crinkled brown rice, firm
and toothsome. Comfort food. To end, golden key-lime pie,
the top studded with slivers of green peel. A mint-filled
chocolate fish swam atop my bill.

While I ate, three men and a lady filed in to fill the next table,
all casually dressed, all but one in their thirties,
and he, a florid man of fifty plus. Perhaps
an office Christmas party from a medical supply house.
They brought little piles of holiday cards
to sign for their customers, each pile
handed to the next person as soon as one had signed.
No matter how they tried, they could not stop talking shop,
and I remembered Christmas parties with other psychologists,
how we always talked about our cases (impossible), our tests
(outdated), and we never could get beyond that, though we'd
all known each other more than a decade.

The phrase "ventricular fibrillation" focused my ears
on the oldest of the office party quartet. He told his table-mates
that the heart was not easily shocked back to beat after
the first minute and by five minutes, shock seldom succeeded.
My mouth trembled to ask how my mother's heart had begun
to beat again fifteen minutes after her brain's crash and burn,
when no kindly person would want it to begin its steady
pumping, its battering of a dry well. I asked only myself,
caught silent, throat clogged with the "Why"s of a decade
stuck relentlessly at the point where my breastbone
moves with my breath, where the wind and rain gather
when my coat flies open, where each day I fall apart.

Massachusetts Landscape

First snow of each season,
I rise to such astonished whiteness
and fear everything
is lost.

Roots are buried
although I cannot hear them
grumbling in their bed of hard earth,
nor any promise of song.

In this impossible silence
I believe
everything with meaning will dissolve,
run off limbs of trees in the midday sun.

Yet nothing is lost:
the great mill of the world will return,
green cloth will unroll from the spool,
weavers will sing.

Physical Examination

There is a gum-ball machine in my head
and a jukebox stuck on "Light My Fire."

My feet try to hurry, stuck in their snowshoes.
The bear in me demands to be filled.

Freezer-burn scars my toes
but my wrists are catalogs of hope.

I could see sleep in anyone's eyes.
I could feel love in the shape of a skull.

Before My Bones Were Set

Before Pearl Harbor flamed,
mother and father perfected desire.
Red dreams swung in her empty shell,
a dark bruise of shared delight.

Neurons flashed as atoms split,
as I became fish and bird and woman.
My cells swelled like ripened fruit
and bones began to form, while my father
sailed into the teeth of war.

In half-light hours she could not count,
my mother cried "Jesus Mary and Joseph"
over and over, although she was not Catholic,
and I was born yelling, with long fingernails,
hands that had to be tied, fontanel soft and fragile.

War swallowed my father.
Mother counted my bones
like the beads of a rosary, tasted rapture
in the sweet pain of my mouth
at her breast.

I Study Marsden Hartley's "Abstraction, 1911"*

Teal blue becomes that car
speeding down Teall Avenue toward the post office,
traffic light beaming a steady red.
Screech of brakes, fishtailing swish of tires on asphalt,
and the car slips backwards up the ramp,
aqua in shadow, the driver filled with gilt.

This disturbs the village history, its monuments
collected on the mayor's lawn. Roofs of houses raise
and lower like louvers, the proper heirs of
blues so dark they train one's heart to deny the eye.
But I digress. It is that car that is important,
that driver, his whole life condensed into one small blur.
He's lost his dog, his wife, his roof. Now the car will go.

Police arrive, their klaxons blaring. These errors
are common occurrence. They blot the landscape
like golden hubcaps. The driver babbles and sobs,
consents to psychiatric sign-in. The sun slides
behind the teal blue roofs which lower and darken.

**Marsden Hartley, 1877-1943, American Artist*

Connie Recounts Her Dreams to the Therapist

I want bread studded with raisins or nuts,
slabs of liverwurst, hills of strawberry jam,
vichyssoise and creme brulée.

Each night I sleepwalk,
traipse between refrigerator and microwave,
or down to Huzzard's Groceteria on the corner.
When rain harries our street, I call
somewhere that delivers – thirty minutes, no delays.
Doggie-bags get raided on my nighttime forays,
left-overs from dinners at Alfredo's or The Brass Rail.

I want pork roast wrapped in its cloak of saran,
gobs of sour cream, curly fries entwined like lovers,
peanut butter, and grits with gravy.

I have grown more solitary.
I clutch my porcelain altar in daily ritual,
lay my cheek upon its cold white rim
and offer sacrifice to this slender God who screams,
"Thinner! Thinner!" who accuses me of lost control.
I scar my throat as penance for sins of gluttony,
that lust for food, better than love, than dreams,
than promises the world never keeps.

I want one box of Omaha steaks, another of duck breasts,
Haagen-Dazs in eight different flavors, all chocolate-something,
Cheez Whiz and Velveeta overload.

When I dress for work each morning,
I catch the mirror, see myself wearing the skin
of a plump pink frankfurter ready to burst at the boil.
Why can't I soothe myself with mouthfuls of hair,
run pearls, wrenched from their rope, through my teeth
and be replete? My hunger turns her head away,
refuses them all.

I want fried rice weeping grease, Lady Baltimore cake,
Buffalo wings swimming in a creamy bleu cheese pool,
A wheel of pizza heaped with meats and stuffed with cheese.

I want to chew whole worlds,
feel them ooze between my teeth,
worry them with an anxious tongue.
I want to swallow my desires,
a warm lake in my belly
filling all the empty spaces, flowing to my heart,
shocking it like static from an old-time radio,
the way it catches a listener unaware.

Grandmother and the Barrel of Rattlers

Avoca, PA (1905)

Flies hung thick around the wagon, dust devils
hissed from the wheels when they drove
to the nearby farm each Sunday after church.

Mr. Wiggins chewed and spat and smelled of cows,
claimed the mare wasn't ready yet for dropping foals.
Her father'd say, "Don't fidget, girl. Go and play,"

breeding not a subject fit for twelve year olds.
"Stay away from the snakes," he'd add, and ready himself
to haggle on prices for livestock and produce.

Out of their sight, she'd run to the barn, shinny up
and lean over the sides of the barrel to see
those snakes squirming, or somnolent, below.

She'd hold their gaze, drawn by their slither and slide,
the rattling gourds in their tails. Each week,
they drew her across the dusty yard. Perhaps she read

the future in their eyes. Perhaps her life depended
on their hooded gaze, promising lies she'd treasure
if she lost her place, her sense of where she was in time.

Someday she will own much and want more. Treacherous
dreams will hide in the barrel. My grandmother
will stretch and coil, stretch and coil.

Waiting for the Ferry

Provincetown, August

A tease at a masquerade, the ocean
wears a disguise – blue dress or gray dress,
ruffles or scallops. Who can predict
her unmasked face? We see only
the approaching ferry slicing its way
across today's unremarkable pattern,
but feel the leashed shuddering, know
the sea's all woman. In an instant,
on a whim, she will break
your shoes and, wherever you are,
she will make you long for home.

Photo Found Caught in the Back of a Drawer

My parents hold hands
as they stand by the garden
riotous with vegetables.
It is 1942 and my mother looks
like the pictures of war brides
you see in old magazines,
sure of herself, sure of her husband,
their future already planned in detail,
if not in the eye of God.
My father stands over her.
She is a bean to his zucchini.
His smile tears holes in my heart
but his ensign's cap casts a shadow
across his face, his uniform
as white as the tombstones
marching across an Arlington lawn.

Fifty-Fifth Birthday Blues

I am approaching the age of my mother's decline
when her veins and arteries shut down,
when her legs couldn't take her
more than a few steps and she needed a pillow nearby,
when the operations came closer and closer in time
and the doctor said he had no other cures.

A decline not of bones but of blood,
the steady highways to and from the heart.
Too much waiting for cars to start their journeys.
Too many misplaced maps, broken watches,
sticky-surfaced roads.

We must have explanations for what happens
in our lives or we would go mad.
But I may be dwelling in a house with dry rot
behind the clean visible boards,
and no explanations will heft fresh wood
or make my house safe haven.

The clocks on my walls have hands
that sweep like my mother wielding a broom.

Without Trees

What if one morning, when we went
down the stairs and out our door,
we could see no trees anywhere,
drive as we might in any direction.

An absence so strong it became a presence.
No maple or pine, no flowering crab. Bushes, too:
the lilacs gone south, forsythia forgotten everywhere,
rhododendron a misspelled word wiped from the language.

Ignore winds, the lack of shelter.
Ignore deserts, a sea of sand.
Ignore the loss of birds.

What cannot be forgotten are scents: resin,
sweet rot of leaves in November, magnolia's edgy
perfume. What cannot be forgotten are bird trills
at dawn, the rub of branches, their rustle, rustle, rustle.

Our souls will shed bark in long splinters.

X-ray

Her body cannot be hidden in dark spaces.
Its bones glow in the dark.
She will rise from her bed, shake herself
like a dog fresh from lake water.

If she looks through the east-facing window
she will see an elm crested with light
her bones have let go. The light deepens
like fire in the belly of a cast-iron stove,
flaming the leaves of that tree,
warming the water-bright dog
frisking beneath its branches.

That dog gambols through beds of late flowers –
marigolds and asters and mums –
eating every purple blossom. More bloom
even as they are consumed.
Her bones flower. Such bright poisonous jewels.

Nineteen Fifty-One

This poem is about being small and powerless,
Holding dolls at night through our small sleep.
In the classroom, we sit like mushrooms
Rare and exotic. Some may fruit. Some not.
Doors to the cloakroom slam shut. Families leave town.

Grade three, fulcrum of childhood. Pigtails grow longer,
Reach for fingers to comb through their knots. How
Awful our terror when the teacher clears her throat.
Desperation makes us wave these little hands.
Everything we know spills from our lips.

My Life with Birds

They time their migrations
from neighborhood to neighborhood

with my daily outings. Each time I leave
my house, they fly by to check.

When I am indoors, they hover
outside my windows, a mix of crows

and starlings, their dirty cousins.
I find myself forgetting to wash.

They chase away wrens
and errant robins to eat scattered seeds.

I know they can change my life
with their curiosity and appetite.

I hear their cry,
their overhead swoop

even through closed car windows
in the bank parking lot.

As I walk to my car,
streams of them fly over,

an unruly mob of chitters and caws
heading eastward toward my house.

Barren

A military metaphor works for men:
he's shooting blanks, they say.

For women, no metaphor will do.
What can you say after all?

Try: iron in the heart, blood-roots
turning green, then blackening,

cold northeast winds that will never
guide you home.

Charlotte Fears for Her Son

I loved pulling each garment onto your wriggly body,
buttoning buttons, snapping snaps, patting down creases,
while your feet churned the floor, wanting to run, to explore
your own green world. Dangers stalked the street
but always, here, there were arms to teach and lips
that spoke of love. There were no secrets between us
and I visioned your future with an unknown
beautiful lady, a safe beautiful life.

Last night I imagined you getting ready for your date:
buffing your shoes to high gloss,
brushing the lapels of your grey suit
with a brisk twist of your wrist,
tying your silk tie, its emerald and topaz birds lifting in flight.
You fastened pearl studs with delicate fingers
as if touching the lover you were going to meet.

I dreamed I saw you, John, through a dimly lit window.
An overhead bulb swayed as your arm brushed it in passing.
You removed that neat gray suit,
untied the hand-painted tie,
pulled your leather belt through its loops,
pants sprawling to the floor, shoes lying

unattended by the door. I saw him
run his fingers over your fair hair, grip,
saw you take him in your mouth

then you were stretched on your bed, the room well lit,
tubes from your nose, bottles feeding you,
catheter snaking from beneath rough blankets.
Your lover sat beside you; I could not see his face.
I have never seen his face.
He has done nothing but weep since you have been here.
He fears it is his fault. He fears for his own life.
But he is nothing to me.

It is you that matters – my son who is not yet sick,
who may never be sick, but every night,
when you walk out that door, shimmering in moonlight,
I wonder how many times luck
will follow you like a shiny coin tucked
in your pocket. When will the eye
in its tiny face blink
just as that dangerous, sick one comes by,
his death-defying ecstasy waiting just for you.

Ethel and Julius

Dog Lake, Battersea, Ont. 1953

Fishing from a rented boat,
my family could hear the loons,
their songs tangled in July sun.
We dangled lines all afternoon,
not urgent now to net our lunch.
We let our minds fly, random birds.

The words burst from my grandmother
without warning. "They say it took five
jolts; she sat bolt upright at the first."
Righteous horror edged her voice.
She finished with "He only needed two."

The Ontario lake a blur, boat's
electric purr a stammer now and then,
I don't remember catching fish that afternoon,
just a ten-year old's vision of Ethel, straining at her bonds,
Julius, next to her, already slumped in the chair.

Derecho*

Trees yawn from earth.

Roots stare at the sky,
promises to endure and give
shade broken, boughs
cut at their base, leaves

plastered to sides of houses
like the beginning of tole painting,
a plate named
"Derecho: What the Wind Left Behind."

September begins this way:

crashes of trees, crush of roofs,
mangled cars in yards as stripped as mines.
When we look up, there is only sky
and wind stars us with loneliness.

It will never marry.

We have survived
torn sky,
night you could read by,
long roads of rain.

**Derecho: severe weather condition marked by high winds.*

Throwing the Bones

Bones rattle in a tin cup.
My future is being read by a dark-skinned woman,
keeper of chickens. Her dashiki is red,
her turban striped; her hands are clever.
She promises to convey all signs and portents
as they are conjured from the twirling bones.

A distant future is not my concern.
I want to know what will happen tomorrow,
if it will snow, if I will need a root canal,
meet my soul mate walking home from the grocery,
catch flu and not recover.

The woman whispers that I must remember
nature's counterweights of pleasure and pain,
balanced like the bones thrown upon the table.
As one increases, another's falls, even as
my own ribs flicker in light
cast by a fading bulb. Her voice flutters on –

I know that five, ten, twenty minutes from now
someone else's bones will lose their precarious balance,
someone who laughs and talks with friends
as I laugh and talk with you,
will forget to breathe,
cast aside his own cage of bones,
and let everything fall with one last throw.

Why I Cannot Give the Piano Away

After my grandmother died,
after the final wearing down of her body's lathe,
that final grate of gears;
after her remains had been taken to the mortuary
and I had come home,
my mother cast open the white louvered parlor doors
at midnight, seated herself at the grand piano
and played, loud and hard, what she knew best by heart,
as if to give her mother a triumphal march home,
as if to hear her chains dispersed by hammered chords
that made the anvils ring.

Birds at Rest

That winter night
crows sat heavy on the stripped
bones of maples. Thick
clusters of tattered dark leaves
cawed their way through hungry hours,
left their droppings like thin
white stigmata
on brick walks.

After geese passed last week
we expected silent quilts of snow,
crumbs tossed to wintering birds,
later a robin
and the green rebellions of spring.
Unprepared for a murder of crows
above our lawn
we were uneasy, uncertain of their intentions.

We cowered under sweat-stained
sheets until they moved on,
leaving us alive
but shaken.
Tonight they come again,
hundreds circling.
Although this time they do not stop,
their caws edge our sleep, shred our dreams.

Lost Babies

little fishes that swam
my inner waters
nine weeks
finned and tailed

how can I call you when all
is made new
how will I know
your eyes
your dew-lapped skin
whether you are he or she

there are no memories
I only recognized
blood
the loss each time

never looking
closely
at the remains
flushing the bowl
compulsively
refusing that dark answer

sometimes I dream
you became luscious fruit
my womb
bursting like purple grapes
wine
for the deceived heart

Above the Dresser

Nana called it "The Strawberry Girl."
The painting hung in my mother's bedroom
during her last painful year.
                                        The child
wore a thick scowl, cherry lips turned down,
eyes about to overflow like the berries
falling from her basket.
                                        Her other hand
gathered her pinafore together
at the hem, brown curls a mass of discord.
I saw no resemblance
                                        but Nana claimed it
exact replica of my mother, an obstinate,
willful child who did not take well
to obedient ways,
                                        this picture
symbol of the child lost within the adult frame,
now shrinking.

Three Hundred and Sixty Degrees

I've watched us all run
in ceaseless circles, small and tight,
around the same flag festooned with streamers,
the same tree swathed in tinsel,
the same scarecrow with a crow
perched on top. And yet

outside this circle, changes flourish.
Grass needles and is cut. Sunrises, sunsets
purple this world. Trees dabble perfume,
dress for work, then go dancing, mad
in carmine with gold trinkets dripping,
sleep lacy sleep in high white beds.

Comets fly, stars fall, Jupiter loses a moon or two.
When I notice the angles of sun,
I am always surprised. The phonograph
spins those old Bing Crosby platters
and Fred and Ginger dance across ceilings
in my dream. I'm whirled into other scenes:

Zulus sharpening spears, bushmen painting cave walls
with clever rabbits, the Chicago fire;
they're all featured here. Breathless, still
running in a circle dance, panting and amazed,
I'm trying to keep my new shoes shiny,
pennies placed just so.

Thirty Years Have Not Passed

Autumn swirls past the windows
of the Hotel Concord and I am bored.
There is no one I know in this crowded room.

But wait! That girl across the lobby wearing
an onyx brooch, could be a college chum, the one
who sat behind me in Spanish class. I'd
recognize her anywhere.

And that girl over there with glasses,
arranging her wares on racks,
spilled coffee on my best madras skirt
right before summer vacation, nineteen sixty-three.
I remember her laugh, spill of her auburn hair.

And that young man toting boxes, cigarette cocked
at an angle, could have been my worst date
sophomore year, the one who threw up on my coat.

If I cross toward them, move into the light,
I will see that they are different.
They couldn't look like this now
with thirty years of living behind them
to blur their faces and spot their skin.

So does my mirror surprise me.

But here's the pity of it.
I know leaves are falling even as I talk,
obscuring the antique sun-dial in the garden
just beyond these curtained windows.

Portrait of an Unknown Girl

from "Portrait of Clara" (B.J.O. Nordfeldt, 1911)

She is my aunt and she is dead.
I wear her skin. In me she is as alive
as the butcher at the corner market.

She wears that inscrutable look
my grandmother called "sly," called "secretive."
Not one of her thoughts shows. Not one of her dreams.

When she dies, there will be no one left to mourn
or bear fruit. Her dust will be drier than dust.
Everyone will be guilty of neglect,

no one innocent in anything they did or did not do.
Scarves of absence will hang from their chimneys,
smoke will obscure the sun's light.

My aunt's skin burns like paper, first from the sun's rays,
then from the fire that cleaves muscle and skin, that layers
the heart into what must go and what remains.

Crows Are Fighting in the Trees Again

I am wakened by their shadows against
my bedroom wall. More crows than I can
count, they swivel from limb to limb.
Great swells of caws become quarreling squawks
as displaced birds jostle feather and wing,
displeased with whatever tree they circle,
whatever branch takes their black, unbroken weight.

They haunt walnuts and scrub oaks lining
our fence, take residence there
by the hundreds in squalling winter weather.
Even now they cluster thickly
on broken branches deformed
by a September derecho, the storm
that changed the city's skyline forever.

When their wings scrawl curses across night's sky,
houses will lose their north wall,
stars will wink out, one by one.
How long will the heavens burn?
How far does the tree line reach before
crows are only patches of black smoke
and branches are sturdy, unbroken by storm?

Night after night I watch spousal abuse, tribal
warfare, mating dance, each exacting detail
shadowed against my bedroom wall.
I must witness how the crows fight
for the ineluctable branch that will
answer all their hearts' mad questions,
how they never find it.

Putting It in Perspective

for Peg

Earth's shadow
slides its slow way past the moon's
pale door, universe made
blue by cold and wind.
Outside the theater, we pause
to watch its deliberate procession.
Twice this year, death
has cocked her fist at us. Now
your father and my friend
see the sun from its other side,
laugh at cosmic jokes we've yet
to hear. It's dark
beyond the marquee. I stumble
and you take my arm to steady me.
Maybe death was just a crooked sidewalk,
a slowly shifting shadow,
a kind hand squeezing a shoulder
the moment
before the lights flashed on.

in memory of Ann Silsbee (1930 - 2003)
and Bernie Sperber (1911 - 2003)

First Glimpsed Under a Bathroom Lamp

It does not seem to be
my own hand. My skin
is not this color,
this dull chartreuse,
yet in a certain light
my veins map the terminus of age,
not blue, but
uncut jade rivers
spied through wisps of smoke.
We do not think "green"
when we hear "vein"
and this astonishes me.

As October Ends

This year autumn lingers, lasts longer
than any since my childhood fifty years ago
when blasts of red and pumpkin fired forever,
leaves fallen to a tumble of crunch beneath sneakered feet
or snarled in my hair.

Wind's a stranger without swagger
as autumn stretches across hill and valley.
No crystal hammers have struck the leaves
struggling to hold branch and heart together.
No witching frost has crisped a leaf
before its time to color's come.

October's winding down like a swinging rope
but the leaves cling to what they have known.
After last night's first snow I found
a tiny maple impaled on piles of white,
holding on to clusters of bronze and scarlet leaves
brighter than the burning bush.

80 Degrees Fahrenheit and the Geese Are Crying

Last night all I heard
were locusts,
the sawing of insect legs
with their late-summer fiddles.

I cleaned house today, boxed
the trifles I haven't needed for years:
paper dolls and picture books,
roller skates and pink toe shoes.

Mid-August streamed past
my window yet I heard
gabble of geese
in a shimmering sky.

As I mopped the kitchen floor
linoleum turned fragile,
flower-pattern diamonds flowed to oval,
delphinium to lily, my eyes
sleepy, too.

Did they feel
winter's incipient chill before
the planet tilts on its axis?

When the planet tilts, the sun takes
on that pointed vacant look, everything
distant, our shoulders not warmed by its rays.
Even now, in the midst
of this extravagance of summer brightness,
I hold my breath, close and stack boxes,
watch the floor dry.

Like all earth's creatures,
we crane our necks forward
then back, turning and turning
in the bright air.

I pirouette slowly in the sun.

Tell me, mother,
Are my toe shoes tied
or will I trip over their ribbons
streaming behind me
in the wind?

Destinations

My losses, incremental,
adding up with the body's years:
Piles of disappearing socks,
Airplane tickets to romantic cities,
suitcase packed and waiting,
Wallets, the last one slid from my car
roof as I carried in laundry.

The slow incursion of loss
as our bodies diminish:
Hand-knit sweaters I haven't worn
for years,
A pair of black fishnet stockings,
Red lace nightgown tossed to the floor
next to a motel bed.

The loss of those bodies we cherished,
parents knowing first what earth
hides from the living:
My father's medals for bravery, the folded
flag, triangular, precise.
A wedding band worn thin with grief.
The map to wherever I'm going.

Late Night, Late September

These are the hours when ears do their work
to the clock's even-handed ticking.
I catch the scrape of my neighbor's trash can
being dragged to the curb, tractor trailers' hum
as they ply the interstate a half-mile away,
refrigerator's gush and shove
as ice cubes crash into their metal tray.

This is when my body plays its old games:
thoughts that slow or speed up,
breaths losing themselves behind my breastbone,
blood's wild waterfall of bluff
and all the sloughing and shifting of bones.
Like marbles rolling in a jar, I hear the cramps
that threaten tomorrow, my left ankle's turn
as I run up the back stair, another hair's fall to silver.

The rustle of a bird's wing
bruises fistfuls of leaves on my front lawn.
Cicadas scratch and rub during long nights
as September crawls toward extinction,
this whole house settling into its concrete shoes.
All the blank stars turn their faces away.

Visiting My In-Laws

The smell of age escapes from closets,
walks from soles of old shoes and many-wintered boots,
nestles on shelves of worn sheets and towels.

It flees the icebox, caked and yellow,
the paper-wrapped freezer-boxes;
smudges the oven; haunts plates, saucers,

pictures of Jesus on the wall,
paintings of angry birds and angular snowscapes,
photos of offspring, none of them here.

The smell seeps through these rooms,
between whispers of doors and their slanting frames,
as if the breakdown of bodies

burrows into chair cushions,
curls in cups like coddled eggs,
and rains from an open book, a dusty cloudburst.

It's lips unkissed
caught in the wilt of it.
It's overripe fruit on the porch,

yellowed linen folded in drawers so long
the cloth has parted its seams,
a bathtub that hasn't seen water for years.

Elegy for the Fallen

Occasional murders
happen in the leafed branches
of our trees. Listen to the hawks, the crows:
Scree, Scree through the orange tumult of autumn.
Our neighbor's dogs scramble past fence-holes.
Squirrels scatter. Another warbler falls
but his mate devours worm and damselfly.

Another hour of light
remains for you to paint clapboards and sills
but you throw down your paints. All that sage green
skimming the grass, all that white! We lock doors
while the dangerous dogs are loose. We lock
arms and eyes, face down the open yawn of loneliness,
thighs tingling with animal joy.

We grow restless when we are confined
although we get used to leaf-rustle, the falling arc
of branches, accustomed to losing birds
to the white burqa of winter, their skeletons unwrapped
and shining. But dark is coming on fast, we cannot
leave our house and the dogs are barking,
the dogs are barking.

My lover reads of freezing rain, of monarch butterflies
flown south but falling from the firs, frozen.
Yards of carpet blazing there

after the rains have ceased. Yards of butterflies,
their soaring days nothing but smears of color,
brittle and unmoving, fading to dust,
fallen rainbows.

And I think of the organ at St. Lucy's,
quiet now. It wears a patina of dust. No one has played it
since the organist sickened, his body shrinking by half, his wit
stilled by the austerity of death.
He'd been a big man, bigger than his life in a small city,
his music as big as his heart. He was loved
by the poor whom he served, by those new to our ways.

On the day of his funeral, less than forty miles away,
another man was buried as well, this one fallen from a mountain,
snow blown backward as he fell, scarlet of his jacket
like a bird or butterfly or October oak leaf, this one
a younger man, full of bravado and rage against the treachery
of nature, as different from the organist as a cardinal
from a nightingale. But they bore the same name.

In our woodland, birds are trilling May songs. The dogs
have been sent away, the house painted. New kittens
litter the yard next door. And although my lover, my neighbors,
stand tall, the Michaels are falling like trees.

In Memoriam Michael Leo Morgan & Michael Corey O'Brien

The Cutting Edge

In all those icy days and nights
my car patrolled the interstate,
first light just climbing surrounding hills
and back again in obsidian dark
lit by the car's own lamps.
Wind cracked its whip, snow fell,
ice crunched or worse became a frozen lake,
the car a spinning top.

One morning, with brittle sun
and air so sharp it cut to breathe,
no purchase anywhere upon the ice,
I clutched the wheel, eyes hurt
by dazzle slicing through thin glass and knew
I had no say in whether I would crash
or spin or safely bring the car to port.
Bridge rails witnessed my face suddenly indifferent,
my body boneless, fleshless, frozen.
The car slid, straightened, still on the road
as if held loosely by invisible wire.

Tonight, far from those slippery roads,
my body older, softer, less accustomed to change,
a catch in my heart's rhythm or an unexpected pang
throws me back in that spinning car, wondering
when the whirling stops where I will be.
My flesh opens to silence, singing of the bones.
Curious yet unaffected, I wait for breath to start again
as I feel those wires cinch my waist and pull me in.

What Happens in September

Half the leaves
lose their quarrel
with frost and hang
like yellow rags.

Fathers oil their rakes,
foresee the deluge
of shapes, their bent
backs' slow ache

as sons oil skates,
apples rounding
where pumpkins hallo
from low vines.

While limber hands
ready whack of pigskin,
teachers search under beds
for briefcases, sharpen pencils

into lasers. Retired teachers
find their eyes turn red
in the cooler weather
and they sleep like snails.

My Ex-Boyfriend Takes Out the Garbage

His car gears up the driveway, grinds to a jerky stop
outside the back door. He leaps the steps,
lifts the blue bin with its week's complaint of cans and jars,
carries it to the curb, then pulls
the plastic trash bags to their place beside them.
Their yellow ties flutter in the breeze. It takes
two minutes, then he is at the door again,
knocking and calling to be let in
and he sounds so happy, I let him in.
He is gaining weight. He is getting a pot belly.
My cats like the way he smells and crawl all over him.
The bolder one tries to unravel his sweater, the one
I gave him that Christmas we visited his parents and I
cried all morning over the way his father swore at him.
We never spent another holiday there. My choice.
He would have gone. I mean, he really would have
sat there and taken it, flipping the pages of a magazine
while his father ranted and called him every nasty thing on
the planet and cursed him for wanting to ask their rich neighbor
to borrow the car for his senior prom. Thirty-two years ago
and the man still chewed that bone.
He'd been a good kid, a decent kid, a hard worker;

he made touchdowns in each weekend's dust,
A's on every test. He hadn't deserved this.
So *his* evasions, *his* lies, *his* inability
to confront opposition: who could blame him?
I used to spin stories about how he had different parents,
nice people who kept a neat house and spoke kindly
to each other, not people who smelled and
complained about lack of sex, not a father who tried
to grab my breasts when I reached for something in the closet,
a man I was afraid of bumping into in the hall on a 2 AM
bathroom run. I knew he slept naked, I just knew it.
Cold walls, bare bulbs, peeling floors, the mother
asleep on the couch with her potty chair beside her
in the middle of the living room. It was more than I could bear.
Now he does chores to pay his debts,
the money I so glibly offered (his taxes paid, his new career).
In those snowbound years, each time
we drove away, resentment cut a wide swathe
in the snow, easy for our tires to follow.

Dinner for One: Philadelphia

I hate Chinese restaurants,
their Americanized, chop-sueyed and chow-meined food
weeping peanut oil, reeking of salts guaranteed to give you
headache. Every shopping plaza, no matter how small,
has such an eatery and I avoid them all. But the Rodin Museum
was closed, skies threatened rain, I was hungry and this place
looked *different*. ***Better.*** The sign proclaimed "Longs"
and a newspaper review plastered to the window promised
nouvelle Chinese cuisine. And the meal was memorable:
sweet and pungent soup thick with mushrooms, its broth
clear and biting, giant prawns with sliced mango,
baby ears of corn, asparagus cuts garnished with thin strips
of deep fried parsnip in a subtle pineapple sauce.
Plus a glass of good merlot.

A man and girl sat two tables away, her back to me.
She had a broad New Jersey accent and deeply bronzed skin.
The man was middle-aged, in business suit and tie,
with harried frown. He talked about her mistakes at work,
how to do better. I heard "doctor-patient privilege" and
"medical records" and "interns." She tried to justify herself,
interrupting, until he became frustrated, said she would never
understand. She whined how she really wanted to hear
everything he had to say but he sighed, "This isn't
about work, it's about you and me," and she accused him
of involving Marla and he snarled that Marla was

none of her business and he was leaving but she wailed
that she hadn't any money so he waited for the bill, both
of them utterly silent, his body half turned away in rejection.

And I wanted to rush over and say, "Here, I'm
a psychologist, let's talk it over," like I wanted to do
that time at JFK when the young mother was beating
her five tired and sleepy children with a belt and
screaming at them not to cry but I had to catch a plane
for London and didn't intervene. Or the time
in the Emergency Room when the little boy threw
a tantrum and his mother complained that he never
obeyed her but I was called to have an x-ray taken
of my battered ankle so hadn't the time to tell her
that consistency was the key. Consistency.
You beat a kid and he cries. You ignore a kid
and he does the forbidden. You ignore your dinner partner
and she knows it's over. I left before their bill came.
Never saw them leave, if she said anything or he did or
how they slunk out of Long's into the Philadelphia dusk
and the peaceful rain, drops falling one after another.

Autumn Bones

Autumn's still-clothed skeleton shambles
past summer, all its gold abandoned soon.
Here in winter, trees will bleach to bone, the wind
whistle in small, hidden branches.

Our hearts pump so strongly,
little engines pinging along for years
without needing to be oiled or wiped with rags,
quarreling with the brain over whose death will count

the most. Spring's flush of green
begins in the heartwood, in the flowing of water
underground, tomorrow's possible flowering.

Bones turn in the soil to feed each new plant and
I marvel that we are so resilient. Sometimes
the heart can't bear it. Sometimes it can.

History Class

Here's that dream again.
This time it is history class I did not go to,
did not read the book,
didn't even buy the book.
It is lunch time before the final exam,
I have a pile of note cards with someone else's writing on them
and I do not even glance at them.
I go to a party, I cry,
try to figure out how I can graduate without this credit.

Always before, when I had this dream,
it was math class.
That I can understand. There is precedent.
Or ballet recital and I had forgotten my shoes,
the hard pink toe shoes with long ribbons
to wind around my ankles
and lamb's wool to tuck in the toes,
situations that caused flutters of breath in the lower chest,
involuntary prayers for success,
where failure was as real as Sunday papers,
as possible as sore and scabby knees.

Does this dream revise my own history
or reflect it?
I know it warns me to scan the notes
that I don't remember taking,
surround myself with smart people who study,
resist crying at parties, no matter
how my eyes burn.
It reminds me that I have survived failure,
to take credit where I can.

The Woman Down the Street

works as a bank teller
and thinks she is turning
into an animal.
It's the cage,
all those little bars,
seeing people always
on the other side.
She fears bank robbers,
store clerks, chihuahuas.

She shops at night
when most of us sleep.
Her arms are pistons,
clearing shelves of soup cans
and cereal boxes
that crash into her shopping cart.
She can't sleep, used up
by her children, husband,
life's ironies.

Yet she trembles when
she proceeds
through the checkout line.
She cannot write checks in public.

Her hand is palsied
when she strokes her card
through the ATM.

The woman down the street
has always lived
in Baltimore
six blocks from her mother
and her church,
the elementary school
where she wore a purple dress
and twirled like a sparkler
on the 4th of July.
A signal of desire
shining into the Chesapeake night,
she looked bright
as sin.

Her Father's Last Visit

for Barbara

She returned from market, arms filled with ears of corn,
peace offering after a slight tiff that Sunday afternoon,
found an empty room, the mutilated pictures,
her father's face scissored from family photographs.

To this day she has heard nothing.
Her children have forgotten Grandpa's blue eyes,
his untidy white hair, the minty scent
of his breath, the way he'd called them "darling."

She always feared it would come to this.
Would not a man who renounced his sisters,
not even send flowers to their graves,
also cast out a disagreeing daughter?

She framed the finest picture in gold thread, hung it higher
so that everyone could see her smiling family,
his face a black hole above his dark suit. She told those
who asked, "This is my father. Such a wonderful likeness."

Carrying the Dead

Our fathers, our mothers, lie safely buried.
Though they may roll in their graves,
they do not rise. Their brows sink lower
into the loam they are becoming, their lips
stretch to speak only to cousins filling the next plot.
We plant narcissus and violets, know how
even now, they want to warn us of what's to come
with our corporeal selves: how arthritis will curl
our joints, how our bodies will waste away
or swell to cushions hard to carry,
how no matter what happens, it will never
be enough to please them, it will never be as much
as they suffered and even now, remember.

Why I Am a Poet

I do not have my twenty-year old body
all those fulsome curves
bones that jutted hips
legs that went on forever
Legs that worked
knees that didn't buckle
surfeit of breath in these lungs

I do not have my mother's arms
around me and I never will again
My grandfather will not bend
to kiss my hair
I will not taste my grandmother's French toast
all eggy on the bottom
I won't call my aunt "Sis" any more

I haven't written the perfect poem
nor prayed the perfect prayer
I haven't found the perfect lover
who will stay
My cats are not my children
but they must do
because there are no others

The man once my husband
swims further and further away
Black holes and stars have taken him
where I can't follow
I haven't kept all my memories
don't know what I can do with what remains
But there is this

Singing at the Execution

Bees crawl through the comb of crumbling mortar,
their hive nested against the fireplace chimney,
silent as honey at night but, every day,
three or four cling to the bedroom window.
They hotly buzz, their bodies battering at the glass.
I kill them easily. Next day,
sixteen beat at the window. Again
I knock them to the floor, where they lie
stunned and dying. Forty more come, then sixty.
I check the Yellow Pages for a name.
He comes after dusk when the bees have all returned,
fills the hive with poison.
As night ascends, stars flinging small darts of light,
the bees grow boisterous,
sing like divas as they die, nerves burning without fire.
Those nearest the inner wall
crawl between old bricks by the hundreds.
They jerk and spasm, too damaged to live,
my bedroom floor a humming sea while the night
answers with its grasshopper scratch, its tree toad harrumph.

Making Music, NYC, Early 20th Century

from a photograph

Her voice is the bird returning to its nest.
That homing sound. That stuttered ache. The guest

sets aside guitar, joins full-throated in the chorus.
The river writes its own thesaurus

of longing while it laps the docks below, its beat
an undertow as plaintive as drum-roll. Fleet

the music hour, speeding toward a glass of sherry,
she passing canapés, he on the ferry.

Summer 1963

And I am twenty again,
in a Gotham hotel room
wearing my tight blue sheath
with its pleated jacket.
I believe I have the qualifications
to become a cruise ship hostess:
I have been a passenger six times
and never suffered mal de mer,
have hostessed at my boyfriend's
fraternity parties with flair and aplomb.
I carry a one-page, self-typed résumé
with three carbon copies.
I am secretly relieved
when they turn me away
but I complain all the way home.

Menopause in March

Her eyes are icy marbles, her skin
a blasted playground of mud and old grass,
her breath a year-round forecast, a dare

to her madcap sisters of green satin lawn
and teacup rain, their dimity snow, their crinkle
of russet and tart-sweet of pear.

Her unkept promises fall away,
strewn like confetti, unkempt and blowsy
with limp, water-logged stalks of hair.

The days seesaw. First the stove is on,
then the refrigerator. All thermostats
demonstrate their need for repair.

Her tongue drips defiance and spittle,
flies like sleet as she plots deeper mud flats,
frosts that wound and strip blossoms bare

of spring promise. It's back to wet stalks'
pale beige that lies by its presence. Endure
days, wrap up your nights. Sniff the air.

She spits out lies like a coked-up whore,
charging us for our bodies because her rent
is due, and after all, we are there.

My uncle lives in an acorn*

because he has gone squirrelly
with venom and age. He has forgotten
his name and his language. He does not
know his wife; sorrow and confusion have
wilted her into a tissue of tears and liniment.
He is in a hospital that cannot contain him.
He attacks the staff and they say it is not
his brain going soft like over-ripe cheese
but a storm coming in from the south.
They will send him to another place,
a larger place where he will be bound
to his chair with rope, the cords
of his neck standing out as he strains
against the bonds of love that hold him here.

**from a line by Michael Dennis Browne*

Early April, Washington Heights

for K.C.

The rattle of trains gives way to brief hush.
In front of me, two large green doors
open into spring, into Bennett Park, forsythia
beginning to lean its golden fever over
wrought-iron railings. Students from Yeshiva
hurry by, books balanced and heavy with learning.

A few late lunchers bolster the benches, busy
with salads or sandwiches, paperbacks half-open.
But the burgeoning flowers cannot be quieted
in their seamless racket. Sidewalks
blaze with children on red tricycles, babies
in prams and strollers, mothers
shrugging off their jackets, throats lifted to the sun.

Moment of Truth

My body lay on your bed but I was not home.
Perhaps I wandered through a laundromat or bank,
bought stamps or a new refrigerator, did
every prosaic thing I have ever done alone.

I returned to find that burglars had broken in
and stolen the poems and the piano,
had broken the pens in half.

And I felt that loneliness after love,
that wind whistling through hollow space
boundaried by ribs and spine, by vertebrae
and berserk beat of heart.

I heard the chatter of children and thieves
wanting to enter that door behind my eyes,
wanting to come home.

Flying to Maine

One man cradles a salmon, rubs his bearded jaw
as he bends and twists his way to a seat.
Two solemn-faced women, obvious Mainers,
navigate the narrow aisle. A third folds into a seat
up front. The plane shimmies and jerks
as we follow the evening tide to Rockland.

Coffee spills down my open collar, the view
all seawater and coves, eelgrass and marshgrass.
We muster our way through fog into sky so big
the airplane cannot contain it. Our hearts
swing like lobster pots
the little boats are set to gather in.

This is not a new unhappiness

It has followed me
everywhere
since the day we met, sea
lapping around our ankles, sun
pulling at our ears.
It whimpers
underneath my pillow
at midnight
when moonlight seeps below
the curtains of my room and crosses
my face with stars,
an animal I could pet
if it were small enough.
If it were starved.

Christmas Eve

Geese, late starters,
honk their way south
all week long.

Winter breathes despite cries
of late birds, sputter of rain,
drafts a poem I must write.

Like all poems,
it will be about bones, how they break
and are set in imperfect, finite lines.

It will be about hours
that blink at the sun,
years combed through our hair like rivers,

and hope, that great white bird
lodged between our shoulders,
how it learns to fly.

She threw the eggs down on the cement

but did she throw them in wrath,
did they hit the ground like exploding grenades,
small pieces of white shell
spread in a wild mosaic over yards of stone,
she a one-woman army advancing,
mouth set but little panting sounds coming with each breath

or did she scatter them in confusion
when a tiny finch fresh from his bath
flew in her ear and startled her
so that all the eggs fell and rolled on the grass,
acres of green lawn speckled with bits of white and yellow
as vole and shrew and raccoon peered from behind the thicket

or did she drop them hurrying up the cellar stairs
like my mother did, eggs
splatting onto each linoleum-covered step
like miniature omelettes ready to be slipped in the pan,
mother crying *Drat you, it's your fault* though
my head was in a book and I hadn't said or done a thing.

Necessary Homework

House of bone

that cannot grant shelter

Lathe of bone

on which her world spins

Knife of bone

caught in the heart's own wormwood

Clock of bone

that strikes hours like matches

Needle of bone

sewing and sewing

Meal of bone

the dog at her table

Wire of bone

arcing from both ends, the little spark, the hiss

Shower of bone

that breaks skin, small rivers of blood

Caul of bone

fine as a veil over her eyes

Book of bone

she must read in the dark

Rosary of Bones

Easy to praise
when it's green and fresh
and the air smells ironed.
Easy to open hands,
spill seeds, tamp soil,
like my grandmother before me
who saw angels in the rain.

Now that I have become
my grandmother
I wrestle with weeds and words,
fling the rake around.
The world has evolved
into a truly stubborn place,
a curse of rocks to trip my feet.

I haven't seen angels for years
and I need them in my garden:
soil with its stony crop,
worms among the roses.
But here I count
the bones that work,
the springing summer hours.

I give thanks for leaves,
for autumn's bronze
and winter's grace:
snow's white confection
erasing even as it is erased.
This peace. This praise.
Amen.

Biography

Jennifer MacPherson is a founding editor of *The Comstock Review.* Her work has been published widely in such journals as *Poet Lore, The MacGuffin, Calyx, Pearl, The Connecticut Review, Louisiana Literature, South Carolina Review,* and *Primavera.* She is the author of a 2002 chapbook, *Stuck in Time* from Pudding House, which also published her *Greatest Hits* (2001), *A Nickel Tour of the Soul (*FootHills, 2004), and *In the Mixed Gender of the Sea (*Spire, 2004), which won the Spire Press Poetry Book Award. A former school psychologist, she lives in Syracuse, NY, with her ocicats, Tango and Samba. In her spare time, she is a gourmet cook, amateur gardener, ballroom dancer, and obsessive reader of everything.

Printed in the United States
200023BV00009B/1-129/A

9 781933 456799